"I started reading your book – which, let me tell you was awesome (it goes right up there with Harry Potter ☺)"
Jasneet, Student – Central Leadership Seminar

"There are some great ideas in your book that he will find helpful. How do I know? (I'm reading the book, too!)"
Joyce, Parent - Michigan

"Your book is brilliant! I have read it almost six times and shared it with members of my student council. As the President of my school next year, I am going to apply what you have taught me."
Ann Marie, Student Leader - Toronto

"I came home after hearing you speak I was talking to my principle about leadership and awesome speakers and right before I mentioned you she handed me your book, which I already bought so I passed it on to another student. He read it and passed it on and Friday someone brought the book to me and said I had to read it!"
Riley, Student that Paid it Forward - Cyberspace

ISBN: 978-0-9811398-0-7

Published by Spetha Inc.
Oakville, ON, Canada

Third Edition 2012

Author: Sunjay Nath

Contact Information:
Sunjay Nath
sunjay@sunjaynath.com
www.ABCsofStudentLeadership.com

TABLE OF CONTENTS

PREFACE

When I was a student and heavily involved in student leadership, I had to learn a lot of things from scratch. On the one hand, this was good because of the firsthand experience I gained. On the other hand, I could have been so much more effective and successful if I'd had a few pointers along the way. In that spirit I have written this book to offer you a few of those tips to help make sure you have an even better student leadership experience. This is a collection of wisdom, stories, suggestions and guidelines. I definitely do NOT know everything, but if my experience can help reduce your learning curve, I am happy to share them. I hope you enjoy it and use it as a tool to create success on your journey throughout high school and beyond.

There are nine key words in this book – three A-words, three B-words and three C-words, hence the title of this book, the *ABCs of Student Leadership*. The nine words are Attitude, Action, Alliance, Balance, Belief, Behavior, Commitment, Change and Character – each forms a chapter in this book. There are many other words that could have made chapters but these nine words summarize the core of what I feel student leadership is all about.

Finally, before we launch the book, let me define what I mean by student leadership. Put simply, student leadership is getting involved. It doesn't matter if you are captain of the soccer team, whether you play left bench or are the water boy (or girl). If you are getting involved and you are part of the team, I consider you a student leader.

Now some of you may be thinking, "Does merely being a bench player on a team really constitute leadership?" My answer is, "ABSOLUTELY!" You'll find one of the themes in this book is that the qualities that form leadership are primarily intrinsic and internal. That means that to be a leader of others, you must first learn to lead yourself. If the best way you can contribute to the team is by being a bench player, then that makes you a leader for putting yourself in a situation where you are part of the team and you are pushing yourself to develop as an athlete.

You will find a section called "Leadership Journal and Exercises" at the end of each chapter. This is an opportunity to actually put into action some of the concepts and ideas from the chapter. No one is forcing you to do them. But keep in mind, you may have all the knowledge in the world, but unless you act on it, it is useless.

Don't be thinking, "Homework, he's giving us homework! I'd rather rub my face with sandpaper than do homework." Instead look for how this can serve you and bring you to the next level of leadership. True leaders sometimes push through things that may seem trite at first and soon realize the importance and value of doing that. Every successful athlete at one point has been frustrated about training. Every successful leader has had the ability to push through even when they don't feel like it because they are having a bad day.

You may want to keep all of the written answers together and form a Leadership Journal. Then when you are feeling lost, or lack direction, you can refer to this and it will give you a sense of guidance and remind you of your strengths and value and how those will help you to achieve your dreams.

One more thing - the best leaders know when it is best to lead and when it is best to let others lead. Leaders know their strengths and allow others to develop theirs. Sitting back and letting someone else have or share the spotlight speaks volumes about you and your character.

Leadership is not only about leading others, it's more about leading yourself - doing your best, stretching your limits and being the best you can be for yourself and for the people around you.

I've been fortunate all my life to have great people around me. I believe that everyone has great people around them and if you don't notice them it's because you aren't looking hard enough. Trust me, they are there. Specifically, I wanted to mention some of the people who were instrumental in helping me with this book project.

So, thank-you, thank-you, thank-you (and did I mention thank-you) to my magnificent editing team and idea-bouncing crew that consisted of Stephanie Stevens, Jacqui Markowitz, Susan Turner and Tina MacLean. I thoroughly appreciate your wisdom, your thoughts and candor.

Dan "the Man" Norman, your cover design is fabulous (that's alright, you can close the book and see what a great job he did. Just remember to come back and continue reading). Thanks for sharing your creative genius. Serena Siu did an amazing job on the illustrations and really helped bring the book to life.

To my wonderful wife, Enette, and our son Zander, thank you for whipping me into shape (I wish I didn't mean that literally). Having you two in my life makes me wealthier beyond imagination. Thank you.

So buckle up and let's embark on the ABCs OF STUDENT LEADERSHIP ...

Sunjay

INTRODUCTION

Some would describe my high school years as "successful." I was heavily involved with many different activities, earned excellent grades, stayed out of trouble (for the most part) and had a lot of fun. (Yes, it is possible to stay out of trouble and have fun at the same time!) In fact, in  my last year of high school, I was Student Council President and Valedictorian, ran the school store, worked for a bank, played volleyball, acted in three school plays with the lead in two, was on the School Reach team, Academic Decathlon, chess club, Project Biosphere, attended seven leadership conferences, missed 120 classes of school (all for school-related reasons – no sick days and no skipped classes) … and I maintained a 95% average (4.0 or A+) in school. I have a very similar resume in college. But when I look back, although I did well academically, I learned a lot more in extracurricular activities than I ever did in the classroom.

Don't get me wrong; I am not saying that I didn't learn anything in classes. Nor am I suggesting that you tell your teachers that you are going to join the basketball team instead of attending school because that's where the real learning goes on. It's not likely that would be received well!

What I am suggesting is there is a balance between in-class and out-of-class activities that will take you much further in your education than academic learning alone.

You just need to find the right balance to really be successful. There's an old saying that goes, "Don't let school get in the way of your education." Since leaving high school, I have found very little need to factor quadratic equations or parse the predicate in a sentence. However, skills I learned in leadership activities have been very useful. How do you learn to work as a unit when two guys on the volleyball team are fighting over the same girl?
What does the student council do when it's an hour before the dance and the DJ hasn't shown up? How does the rest of the cast rally together when someone on stage forgets his line? I have found these skills to be far more useful in everyday situations. If you are already involved in student leadership, great!

I encourage you to continue and where possible grow your involvement. For those of you who are not involved, I would highly recommend you consider participating, as it will enrich your school years and it's a great investment in your future. After all, look how cool I turned to be.

Caveat

Okay, I have to say this because it is very true: you are a student first! That means classes first. Joining clubs, teams and student councils and governments are a bonus, icing on the cake.

If you can't handle the school workload and extracurricular, your focus should be on school until you have enough of a handle on things to take on other projects. School *always* comes first.

I mentioned that I missed 120 classes of school in my last year of high school. Of those 120 classes, guess how many times I told my teachers I wouldn't be in their classes? None. I always *asked* them. I am a student first and then an athlete, artist, actor, teammate, etc.

After seeking permission to miss a class from a teacher (and getting it), the next words out of my mouth were always, "Thanks. Now, should I get the notes from you, or someone else in the class?" It is a matter of respect, to your teachers as well as yourself. If I was missing the class, it was my responsibility to get the work. It was not the teacher's job to run after me.

No, really, it is not! I found that when I was respectful of my teachers, they were respectful of me. I always had permission to miss a class – sometimes they even let me miss tests.

And it was my responsibility to find out how to make that test up. It's all a part of student leadership.

So as you embark on your school journey, it is your responsibility to find out the perfect mix of extracurricular and school related activities for you. Don't worry if you go through times where you feel stressed because you have taken on too much or bored because you haven't taken on enough. Part of the fun of school is to find that perfect balance to get the best out of your scholastic career.

ATTITUDE

"A is for Attitude, which ought to be right; it harnesses skills and preps you for flight."

Many years ago, I met a guy who was talking about leadership. He suggested that we were all student leaders. I found this to be a bit of a stretch - how can everyone be a leader? We can't all be good basketball players or great chess players. Not everyone possesses the skills. Interestingly, the next question he asked was, "Is leadership a skill or an attitude?" Most of the group agreed that leadership is a skill. He then asked us to describe some of the attributes of a good leader. We started giving answers like:

> Enthusiasm
> Patience
> Communication Skills
> Positive Attitude
> Charisma
> Ability to Motivate
> Creativity
> Persistence
> Listening
> Desire to Achieve

 Next, he went on to explain that years of research and studies had been done to determine whether leadership can be taught or if it is something certain people are born with while others are not. In other words, is leadership genetic or generated, nature or nurtured?

The man looked at our list and hummed and hawed for a bit before asking, "Are you happy with this list? I know that we could spend a whole bunch more time making it exhaustive, but for the most part, do you feel that this encompasses what leaders are about?"

We agreed that if an individual had these qualities, he or she would more than likely be a good leader. "Okay," he said. "Most of you agreed that leadership is a skill. Let's revisit this list of leadership qualities and decide whether each particular attribute is an attitude or a skill."

This is what we voted:

Enthusiasm	Attitude
Patience	Attitude
Communication Skills	Skill
Positive Attitude	Attitude, obviously
Charisma	Attitude / Skill
Ability to Motivate	Attitude
Creativity	Attitude
Persistence	Attitude
Listening	Skill
Desire to Achieve	Attitude

The results of our mini survey: 75% of leadership is attitude. That blew us away! It was the first time that I realized that attitude is a cornerstone of leadership. You may have all the skills in the world, but with no desire to transform them into action, those skills are useless.

Attitude is the desire to turn skills into action.

The reading that I've done, coupled with my experiences, tells me that leadership is a healthy combination of both attitude and skill. We are all born with some leadership ability and it is up to each of us to harness that ability and nurture it into something greater. Some of the greatest sports figures of our time are born with a great aptitude and talent (skills) for their sports, but it is more than mere natural ability that makes them successful. It is a combination of both giftedness and hard work. But which is more important? That little poll we conducted suggests that attitude is actually more important than skill.

Because skill without attitude is useless. Consider my friend Pete. In 8th grade, in front of his entire class, Pete's teacher said, "Peter Attia, you are the biggest loser in the history of this school!" (How's that for a supportive teacher?!!)

In 9th grade, Pete was arrested for shoplifting. Through 10th and 11th grades, Pete just got by. In fact, in the summer of 11th grade, Pete received his report card, and calculated his average. It was a whopping 56 percent (a solid D or a 1.1). The truth, though, was that Pete was quite happy with this accomplishment. He had no interest in school, and the fact that he was passing was actually a great achievement for him.

After some thought, he decided that his 11th would be his last year of school. He didn't need it. It was a waste of his time and the teachers', and really they just got on each other's nerves. Besides, Pete knew what he wanted to do with his life and it didn't require school.

Pete trained extensively in Tae Kwon Do and boxing and he decided to be a professional boxer. And he knew that, to be a prize fighter, you don't need any diplomas, certificates or degrees. What you need is to be a good boxer – and Pete was good. So he was quite satisfied with his decision to drop out of school.

That summer after 11th grade, Pete trained every day. He endured rigorous workouts, ate properly and worked hard. One day, he was pounding away on the heavy bag and he suddenly thought to himself, "Wait a second. Not all boxers make it. Some hit the big  time, but for every one of those, there are hundreds that don't make it. Perhaps they aren't skilled enough, or maybe they don't get the lucky breaks, or maybe they get injured along the way. Or they just can't take the disciplined lifestyle." Pete continued to think about his situation. He knew he was good, but he also knew that he might not make it all the way, perhaps even owing to circumstances beyond his control. So he decided that it would be best to come up with a backup plan.

But the only contingency strategy Pete could think of was school – and Pete was definitely not the scholarly type. He thought about his disastrous 11th grade year and tried to justify why he had done so poorly. "C'mon, it's school. Who takes school seriously? I'm sure I could have done better if I had tried harder. If I'd worked as hard at school as I do at boxing, I could get way higher marks. Oh, well." And he went back to pounding away at the heavy bag.

A few days later, after Pete had time to ruminate on his backup plan, he decided what he was going to do. He was going to go back to school and complete his high school diploma, just in case boxing didn't work out. To make things a little more worth his while, Pete vowed that this time he was going to try at school. He was going to do some of the things he did in boxing for school. So what he did was set a goal for himself. It was simple - a 90% (A or 3.6) average in his final year of high school.

Most people encouraged Pete to go for this goal. But no-one really believed he would come close to achieving it. But Pete was motivated by everyone telling him to "go for it," "write down your goals" and "put your mind to it," and so he did. He decided which classes he was going to take and the goal he wanted in each. Then he wrote them down.

He had heard that "Algebra and Geometry" was a difficult class, so he set a goal of 88%, and since he felt he could be a strong English student, he set a goal of 92%. The average of all the marks was 90%. He took this goal sheet and placed it in his desk drawer at home.

Off he went to school with a very different focus, a different attitude than he had ever had before. His goal was to learn, to achieve and to get that 90% average. He tried doing things he had never done before at school ... like going... asking questions ... studying ... and – get this - EVEN writing tests.

His first test of the school year was Algebra and Geometry. When he got it back, he had to do a double take at the score. The test had Pete's name on it and a mark that read 89%. Pete rushed home and pulled the goal sheet out of his desk. He changed the goal for Algebra and Geometry from 88% to 89%. Why? Because now it was a realistic goal.

As the semester went on, Pete kept referring to this goal sheet and making alterations. Sometimes he moved the marks up a little, and sometimes he even brought them down, always trying to keep them as realistic as possible.

Midterm of first semester arrived and the students got their report cards. Pete calculated his average and almost passed out when he realized he had a 92%. He had crushed his goal. In his excitement, he headed to his guidance counselor's office.

"Mr. Callahan, I'm gonna win the Governor General's award." Pete bragged. (The Governor General's award is similar to a lot of schools' Valedictorian; it is awarded to the student who graduates with the highest average.) Mr. Callahan responded, "Pete, you had a good half semester – way to go. But Jennifer Robinson is at 94%. That's miles ahead of you; let me be realistic for a moment. You aren't going to win, she is." Pete was crushed and angered. As he left to leave Mr. Callahan's office he quickly whirled and said, "Mr. Callahan, you're wrong!" Pete kept on doing what he was doing - studying, goal setting, and working hard.

By the end of first semester, Pete was at 94% as well, tied with Jen Robinson.

At that point, Pete decided a couple of things. He thought to himself if writing down your goals works for school, perhaps it would work for other areas of his life too. Pete decided to divide his life into four areas. He then spent four dollars on four sheets of Bristol board, probably one of the best investments of his life.

 He labeled each sheet: Academics, Athletics, Social and Spiritual. And, just as he had done with his school goals, he wrote down objectives for each of the four areas of his life. Under Academics, Pete wrote down his goals from the original goal sheet that was tucked away in his desk drawer. Now on the Bristol board, it was displayed larger than life.

Under Athletics, he wrote down physical goals; he wanted to be able to bench press a certain amount of weight and he wanted to be able to do the splits across two chairs. He was weird, but hey, he had goals. Under Social, he wrote down goals about spending time with his little brother and sister, as well as with his girlfriend. And under Spiritual, he listed goals that were specific just to him.

Every time he would walk into or out of his room, he would see what was important to him looming in front of his eyes. As before, the goals were not permanent. He made changes, crossing things out and writing in new things, so it wasn't always pretty. The important thing was that it meant something to Pete. He also made another decision. He was going to apply to universities and colleges. Why not? After all, he had the marks.

Midterm of second semester, Pete's marks went to the schools he was applying to - his average was 96.1%. At the time, his favorite radio station was Hitz 97.7 FM. He thought to himself … "Hmmmm, 97.7 … sounds like a new goal!"

So his new goal was to graduate high school with a 97.7% average. When all was said and done, Pete graduated just shy of that number. He graduated high school with a 97.3% (an A+ or 4.0), won the Governor General's Award and went off to study Engineering at Queen's University. The year that Pete entered his program, Queen's had a higher cut-off average than Harvard. He was studying in a program that had an 80% failure rate. How did he do? He graduated with a degree in <u>Mathematics and Engineering Applied Mechanics Option</u> with a 91% average. Then Pete decided that he didn't want to be an engineer.

So he went back for another year of university and picked up some Anatomy, Biology and Biochemistry credits. Then he applied to medical schools like Harvard, Yale and Stanford. They say that Stanford is the most difficult medical school in the world to get into. An average of eight thousand people apply each year and they accept about eighty.

Pete went to Stanford and graduated near the top of his class. Then he moved to Baltimore, Maryland where he studied as an intern at John Hopkins University where he specialized to become a cardiac surgeon. Right from

8th grade, Pete possessed the skills that have allowed him to be successful.

It wasn't until he was pounding away on a heavy bag after dropping out of school that he changed his attitude about school. His change of attitude is what allowed him to marshal his skills to be successful.

As you attempt projects and take risks, remember that it is your attitude that will take you much further than your skill. Having a positive attitude when things look bleak, being able to walk away from failure with an outlook that says you've learned something for the next time and having a willingness to embrace new people and new ideas: these things will carry you to many successes.

LEADERSHiP JoURNAL AND EXERCiSES

Here it is, your first chance to start taking action and actually improve your leadership skills, rather than just talking or thinking about it.

In this section, I will offer activities that will reinforce the concepts we just chatted about. Some of you will choose to ignore them and some of you will push yourself and do them. That will separate the followers from the great leaders. So let's start.

1. Make a list of all the qualities that you think makes a good leader. Try and make the list at least 25 items long. Feel free to use the ten I provided at the beginning of this chapter to help get you started.

2. As we did earlier in the chapter, go through and identify each of the 25 items as either an attitude or a skill. If you are unsure or divided, call it both.

    Then tally up attitudes and skills and see for your definition of leadership how much is attitude and how much is skill.

3. Identify which items of the list of 25 that you currently either do (attitude) or possess (skill).

4. Write down two ways you can start to harness and develop items on the list that you don't currently have.

5. How would your best friends describe you if they were asked? What type of attitude would they say

you have? If you are unsure, ask them. Is this consistent with how you see yourself?

6. What attitudes do you currently hold that you feel might be preventing you from succeeding to your fullest potential? What can you do to reduce or eliminate those attitudes?

7. What attitudes do you currently hold that you feel will help propel you to succeeding to your fullest potential? What can you do to foster and grow those attitudes?

8. As an experiment, the next several times you are interacting with total strangers, at a mall or grocery store for example, take note of how your attitude will affect the way people treat you. Try using different personas to deal with people for example try being aggressive, or shy, or mean, or polite. Then answer this question: when you are trying to achieve a goal, what is the best attitude for you to use?

ACTION

"A good plan today is better than an excellent plan tomorrow."

■ US Army General

Getting involved truly does make school fun. It's also an outlet for stress, and it's where you will make some of your best friends. In high school, one of my teachers was trying to sound very profound and philosopher-like and he said to our class:

"Remember, wherever you go, that's where you'll be!"

The class had a good chuckle and we went back to what we were doing. It was silly, but so obviously true. Or was it? I can't argue that physically, wherever you go, that's where you are – but mentally, I think it's all too often a different story for some people.

I've done it countless times. There were occasions when I had a big assignment due, or a test to study for and my friends convinced me that we really needed to go to see a movie. My rubber arm was twisted and off I would go! But the entire night would be ruined by this overwhelming sense of guilt that I hadn't stayed home to do my work. Not only would I not get my homework done, I wouldn't enjoy myself because I was too busy worrying about the work I wasn't doing. I lost twice.

Other times, in similar situations, I held my ground and stayed in to do my work, only to find my mind constantly straying, wondering what all my friends were up to. Again, I lost twice; I wasn't productive with my work because my mind wasn't on it and I didn't get to go out with my friends.

So although it seemed obviously true, it wasn't completely truthful. Too often, we are someplace physically but mentally, our mind is wandering. To avoid the double-loss syndrome, I have made a slight revision of my teacher's attempt at wisdom: "Wherever you go, be there!"

It doesn't matter whether you are doing homework, watching a movie, or taking out the garbage. If you have decided to partake in an activity, give your entire self and be committed to it, regardless of how trivial you think it might be. When you are taking the dog for a walk, enjoy the walk and take in the fresh air. When cleaning your room, don't just go through the motions; go through the emotions as well. This is why we often forget things. For example, physically we place our keys somewhere but mentally we aren't paying attention. Be mindful. Be fully present. It's really more interesting here than in la-la land.

When we aren't both mentally and physically in the moment, we miss out. Once, in late October, I was driving home from a presentation in Niagara Falls and I got lost. I became frustrated because I was supposed to meet up with some people and unless I found my way rather quickly, I was going to be late. As minutes passed, I grew more and more agitated. At one point, I started banging my steering wheel yelling at a red light to change so I could be on my way. Needless to say, the light did not listen to me. Eventually, I ended up in a place called Niagara on the Lake, not that far from

29

where I was trying to go but distant enough to boil my blood.

For people that have never heard of Niagara on the Lake, it is one of the most beautiful places in North America. It is known for quaint bed and breakfast inns, lovely parks, gorgeous scenery and its famous wineries. There I was, passing through this picturesque setting during late autumn, when the leaves had changed and the weather was perfect – and I was hitting my steering wheel and yelling at traffic lights. My freaking out didn't help me arrive sooner, but it did make me miss out on the stunning beauty of Niagara on the Lake.

So wherever you go, *be* there!

The same holds true for school activities. There are too many people who join clubs for the sake of padding their resumes and don't have any real desire to make a difference or truly help. They are physically part of the team or club – but mentally they are elsewhere. I urge you not to be one of these people. If you are committed and genuinely want to get involved, you will always get more out of the team or club than someone who doesn't care.

And the same goes for anything you do in life.

It is simply a matter of desire. When you have a desire to take action, not only will you do it, but you will enjoy the journey. Don't do it because you 'have to' but because you want to. Don't HAVE to, GET to. What I mean by this is so many people do things because they feel like they are forced to. People say things like "I HAVE to go to work," "I HAVE to go to school," "I HAVE to take out the garbage." But can you see how things fundamentally change when you GET to? The phrases, "I GET to go to school," "I GET to go to work," and "I GET to take out the garbage" imply that you are grateful for the opportunity. There are millions of people around the world that would love education, work or a community where there is garbage pick-up. When you GET to do something, you enjoy every moment of doing it. Do you HAVE to go on a date with that really hot guy or girl, or do you GET to?

Action is about the quest to do, to create, to grow and to succeed. Often the hardest thing to do is to take the first step. The most difficult meeting to show up to is the first one. It can be intimidating and scary. But once you can clear that initial hurdle, the rest gets easier.

When I was in grad school, I took a course called Change Management. In that class, our professor told us about a study researchers had done on abandoned buildings. I'm not sure why they were researching abandoned buildings – but I digress.

They found that, in general, once a building became abandoned, it would often take considerable time for a window to break, whether through vandalism or weather– sometimes weeks, sometimes months and sometimes even years. Here's the interesting part of the research: once the first window broke, all the other windows would be broken in a relatively short period of time. The longest time between two windows breaking

was always the 0ᵗʰ window and the 1ˢᵗ. Then, the rest followed quite quickly.

There is something that is engrained in our human hard-wiring that says, "Hey, if everyone else is doing it, I can do it, too." That's what happened with the windows: when none were broken, no one did anything. But, as soon as one broke, people started breaking others. The toughest window to break is always the first one.

Don't get me wrong, this is not permission to go around and break windows under the guise of some warped leadership experiment. What I am trying to say is surround yourself with people who are doing the things you want to do. Have you ever been to a play or musical that was only "okay" but at the end everyone gave them a standing ovation?

And even though it wasn't worthy of a standing ovation in your eyes, you still stood up and clapped? Well that's how it works. One person jumps up and starts clapping, and everyone else follows. The hardest thing to do is be the first person. Once you get the first one of anything under your belt, the rest becomes easier. Ask someone who has made a New Year's resolution to start running – the first run is always the hardest. Once you can get over the initial hump, things become easier.

This is also true when taking action in various activities. The beginning is the toughest - attending the first meeting, taking on your first project, playing that first game or doing that first sit-up.

It has been said that a journey of a thousand miles begins with the first step. As you become familiar with your role and abilities, it becomes much easier to take action that creates an impact. Don't be intimidated by new roles. Welcome them and rise to the challenge to make a positive difference in your school, in your community and in your life.

School can be a difficult place. I came across a survey in a magazine by George F. Wills. It highlighted the most common problems facing schools in two eras:

20th Century
- Talking
- Chewing gum
- Making noise
- Running in the halls
- Getting out of line
- Wearing improper clothing
- Putting garbage in the wastepaper basket

21st Century
- Alcohol abuse
- Drug abuse
- Pregnancy
- Suicide
- Rape
- Robbery
- Arson
- Gang warfare
- Assaults
- STDs

Times have changed ... dramatically. That's why it is more important than ever to get involved and to make things better. Get involved in student government, in sports and in the arts. The more students use their time constructively, the fewer problems we will have with things on that second list. Whatever activities you choose to undertake, do them with your whole mind and body, whole-heartedly and with a burning desire!

LEADERSHIP JOURNAL AND EXERCISES

Here we are again, Leadership Journal and Exercises. Right now are you thinking, "Seriously Sunjay, Do I HAVE to do work?" or are you thinking "I GET to do work that will help me develop and grow!" I've heard that 80% of people do not read past the first chapter in a book. If that is true, that puts you in the top 20%. And, if you are actually taking the time to do these exercises that would put you in even more elite company of the general population.

1. If you have not completed your Leadership Journal and Exercises from the previous chapter, please do that first.

2. Make a list of five small things that you have been procrastinating (for example, completing the questions from Chapter One!). These should not be grandiose tasks, but smaller ones – you know, the type that you've been putting off forever and when you finally do them you think to yourself, "that wasn't so bad, why didn't I do that sooner?"

3. Do the entire list from #2.

4. Make a list of five large things that you've always wanted to do. Think of them as hairy, scary goals! Perhaps it is to save up a certain amount of money, or learn to play a sport, or get a job, or learn to speed read, or get an A in math. This list should be things that YOU'VE always wanted to do, not a list of what someone else had told you to do.

5. Take the list from #4 and break down each item into smaller more manageable steps. Then break down each of those steps into smaller steps. Keep breaking things down until you get to the point where you realize that you can take an action today that will move you toward that goal. Here's an example:

Goal: Save $1000

Steps to get there:
  a. Get a decent paying job
  b. Save 20% of each paycheck
  c. Get a high percentage savings account
  d. Save $500
  e. Celebrate!

Breaking down the steps further:

a. Get a decent paying job
  • Write down a list of all my skills
  • Make a list of all the places I'd like to work
  • Buy a newspaper or surf the web for employment opportunities

b. Save 20% of each paycheck
  • This is a simple enough step that it doesn't need to be broken down any more. That means that for ever $100 I make in my job, I will deposit $20 into my savings account.

c. Get a high percentage savings account
  • Research (web or ask someone) which account would be best for you to open
  • Go to the bank and open the account

    d. Save $500
- Agree to stick to the plan to save 20% of each paycheck
- Be patient

    e. Partay!!

6. Once each item is broken down into manageable steps, take the actions and start moving toward that big, hairy, scary goal. You will realize that when you break it down it is not so scary anymore.

7. Psychologists say that an action repeated for 28 days will form a habit. Push yourself for the next 28 days to do something everyday that normally you would push off. For example, exercise, homework or brushing your teeth☺. You will thank yourself for this, and so will your teeth. Not to mention your friends.

ALLIANCE

"Surround yourself with good people and be the best you can be, for yourself and for those around you."

As much as I hate to admit it ... our parents were right – birds of a feather do flock together. It's actually a Catch-22. Birds of a feather do flock together ... but also, because birds flock together, they become birds of a feather. Does that make any sense?

We often associate with people because they are similar to us in one or in many regards. However, when we spend time with people who are dissimilar to us, we will learn from and teach each other things that will make us act similarly in various circumstances.

My mom used to subscribe to a magazine called Bits and Pieces. I remember reading a story in it about a little boy that went to the local ice cream shop to treat himself to some ice cream. He raided his piggy bank for a handful of change and made his way to the store. The clerk paid little attention to this kid until he tugged at her dress and asked, "Excuse me, ma'am, how much is ice cream on a cone?"

"Fifty cents," she answered and went back to the task of clearing tables.

The boy scratched his head and then dove into his handful of change, counting and mumbling to himself. A few moments later, he emerged to ask another question. "Excuse me ma'am, how much is ice cream in a bowl?"

"Thirty-five cents," came another listless response. Once again, the boy examined his pile of change. "Ma'am, can I have one of them ice creams in a bowl?"

The lady went to the backroom, returned with a bowl of ice cream and basically threw it at the kid. She was far too busy with her own 'stuff' even to be polite to this child. The kid ate his ice cream and smiled ear-to-ear when he went to the lady to pay her the thirty-five-cents. He said, "Thank you very much. Have a nice day," and he was on his way.

A few minutes later, the lady went to clean up his bowl when she found a fifteen-cent tip.

She realized how rude she had been to the boy, yet he still left her a tip instead of getting the ice cream cone. Why did he do that? I'm willing to bet that he didn't pull out a calculator to determine what 15% of the total cost of the bill would be; after all it is customary to leave a 15% tip.

He left a tip because that is something that he learned from his mother, or father, or old sibling, or aunt or uncle or someone that had influenced him. He had been socialized to understand that, when we go out to eat, it is customary to leave a tip for our server. He would then pass that lesson on to the people around him and as a result, the people around him would continue the practice. The bottom line is that we need to be aware of our associations and the alliances we forge. Like it or not, we tend to be a product of the people we spend time with. We are constantly learning from and teaching each other. That means we should choose to be the best person we can be, not only for ourselves but also for the people around us that we influence.

What behaviors are you engaged in that you would want others to learn from? How can you share these with others? What behaviors would you be better off to eliminate? Why don't you, then? If you are unclear whether a behavior is appropriate, consider these three tests: TV, Mother and Gut.

The TV test poses this question: If your actions were broadcast on TV and millions of people were watching, would you be proud to say that's you? If you wouldn't want to be seen, then you should probably alter your behavior.

The Mom test is: What would your mom say? Would she approve? Would she brag to her friends about the wonderful things you are doing?

The Gut test is simply answering the question, "Does it feel right?" As human beings, we have an amazing, unerring intuition, and we often ignore it. I'm not saying that every action should be based on how it feels, because almost every child fails the Gut test when it comes to candy, for example, but it should be intrinsic to the decision-making process.

Since we are constantly teaching each other, why don't we try to learn and teach our best behaviors? This point became very obvious to me several years ago when I was running a session at a conference.

Weeks before the conference, I was asked to come and chat with a group called "Teens Tackling Tobacco." They asked me to address the topic of peer pressure. After wrestling with a definition, I decided that peer pressure is when people do something that their peers are doing without really thinking about it.

I really wanted to explain this point, and in consultation with my friend Brian Dallaway – yes I have friends, mostly imaginary, but some real ones too and I'm not saying which kind Brian is – we came up with a great exercise that perfectly illustrates the point. When I walked onstage, I brought four chairs with me. At one point in the talk, I asked for four volunteers to come up there with me.

When they joined me onstage, I asked the four to stand in front of the four chairs. I then launched into a story. When I got to a certain word in my story, three of my volunteers sat down – and the reason they sat down was that I had cheated.

Before the presentation, I had selected three volunteers whom I had prepped. I told them that I would call for volunteers during my presentation and that they  would have to come up and stand in front of a chair until I said the "code word." At that point, they were to sit. They all agreed.

The fourth one had no idea what was going on. So when I said the 'code word', the three prepped volunteers sat down. Guess what the fourth volunteer did? She immediately sat down. Why?

It made perfect sense, from her point of view, to sit down. The chair was there. Everyone else was sitting down. Why wouldn't she? Her response was virtually automatic. Now, similarly, how many times have we been influenced by the people around us to sit, as it were, and we do so without even thinking? I've been to far too many parties where people have used this same 'sit-down' logic. The beer was there. Everyone was drinking. Why not drink? The cigarette was there. Everyone else was smoking. Why not smoke?

Here are the two key lessons of the exercise:

1. It is perfectly okay, and often, in fact, desirable, to be the only one standing.
2. Just as you compel the fourth person to sit down, you can also get him to stand.

The only way to get people to act one way or another is to model the behavior you want them to act. Your alliances with others will get you to stand or sit and often you won't even think about it.

We need to be aware of the fact that people around us are constantly 'standing and sitting'. They will influence us – both positively and negatively. This is why we

must be aware of our alliances. To surround yourself with good people from whom to learn good things is one of the fundamental keys to success.

Peer pressure does not end once you graduate high school or college. If anything, the pressures increase. I wanted to prove this point to myself. A few years after speaking to the "Teens Tackling Tobacco" conference, I was asked to address a health unit that included an audience of doctors, nurses and other health professionals. In the course of my presentation I asked for four 'volunteers' of which three were prepped like the chair-demonstration assistants. I brought these four onstage and began to tell a similar story.

Unbeknownst to me, the fourth, true volunteer, the one who didn't know what was happening turned out to be the Director of Health for the region. He was a gentleman in his 50s, well educated, a leader and most decidedly his own person.

What happened? I said the 'code word' and my three volunteers sat down, just like they were supposed to. The Director of Health looked to his left, to his right and, surprised, said, "Hey, he told us to stand."

When they all ignored him, he said "Alright," and sat down too. He recognized that what he was doing was 'wrong' but he still did it. Sometimes we give in to the crowd even though we recognize that it isn't the best choice. The easiest way to avoid this is to surround yourself with a team of people that will influence you positively. And you return the favor by positively influencing them.

45

 **LEADERSHIP JOURNAL AND EXERCISES**

If you haven't already done so, I suggest that you keep all your answers to the chapter questions together. This will be very helpful for future reference. And if you are doing these exercises on the computer I suggest you print out a hardcopy to keep somewhere where you will see it and be reminded, like your locker or bedroom. Use your Leadership Journal to chart your progress on your leadership journey.

1. If you have not completed your Leadership Journal and Exercises from the previous chapter, please do that first.

2. Make a list of all the friends in your inner-circle and for each person on that list write down two or three keywords that would best describe their personalities. Try to be accurate and use both "good" terms and "bad" terms. Don't think that just because they are your friends that they are perfect.

3. Do the traits that best describe your close friends serve you and push you toward the type of person that you want to be? Or do they pull you away? Or do they do both? You will likely find that they do both, there are times when they help you and times when they hinder you.

To really leverage the Alliance concept best, you need to decide when it is best to be with your friends and when it is best to surround yourself with others. I'm not suggesting you ditch your friends because they are not serving you (although there are times when this is a good idea because if friends are not serving you and helping you grow, they are not really your friends). I am suggesting that sometimes your friends are the perfect support you need and sometimes you are best to get your support from other people or in other forms.

4. In what ways do you influence the people around you? Do you help people move toward their goals or do you deflate them and pull them away?

5. What are three things that you currently do that aren't being supportive of your friends and family? What can you do to change these behaviors?

6. What are three things you are currently doing that support people and help them grow? What can you do to continue and nurture these behaviors?

7. Make a list of mentors and idols that you have respect for in different areas of your life. You don't necessarily need to know the person. What can you learn from these people that will help you? What traits do they possess that got them to where they are today? Who do you know in your life that has these traits? How can you learn to practice these same traits?

8. Over the next 28 days, make a conscious effort to surround yourself with people who are more ambitious than you in certain areas. For example, if you slack on your homework, befriend people who constantly take action to do homework. Remember, all the knowledge in the world is useless unless you take action on it. Don't wait for what you feel is the perfect moment because now is just as perfect

a moment as ever. Forge alliances with those around you who understand this and will help you grow.

BALANCE

"A combination of a plan, patience, the right balance and the same little standard pieces of life that make it possible."

Does the smartest kid ALWAYS get the top mark on every test?

Does the most talented team ALWAYS win the championship every year?

Does the most qualified person ALWAYS get the job every time?

The answer to these questions is NO. To have only one dimension of skill will never yield the results you want. Being the smartest kid does not ensure success. Let's say you know everything. If that's all you have going for you, you still might not be successful.

What if you handle stress really poorly and, although you have mastered the material, whenever it comes to the big test you get all flustered and give the wrong answers? In that case, being the 'smartest' kid would certainly not be sufficient to achieve the highest grade.

We see this all the time in professional sports. One team will spend millions of dollars to attract the most talented players. As a group, they may have the most talent, but they still may not win the big championship. Why not? Because they are one-dimensional – they focus way too much on individual talent and not enough on, say, teamwork. They lack balance.

The individuals, groups and teams that are most successful are the ones that have a healthy balance in whatever they do, between work and play, individual and group efforts, creativity and convention, and athletics and academics.

In our society, there's an age-old stereotype about the 'dumb jock.' But the next time the Olympics are on and the commentators provide the background of some of the athletes, you will be surprised how many of these 'jocks' are actually medical students, lawyers and engineers. The truly successful jocks are very intelligent people. They embody an impressive mix of academics and athletics. They have balance.

When you find the right balance for yourself in whatever path you choose, you generate a crossover effect. That means that success in one area of your life will spill over into success in another area of life. The opposite can happen, too. When things aren't going well, they seem to not go well in all areas. The key to mastering all the things that are important to you is balance. The way you balance your key areas is as unique as your fingerprint. What might be too much studying for you may not be enough for me. Keep that in mind as you look for your optimal balance. Like your fingerprint, it is unique to you.

Sometimes, when you are over-doing something, you need to take a break – if you only have a one-dimensional skill, there is nothing to do while taking that break. If your life is all about basketball and you live, eat and

breathe basketball, it's hard to escape it. Instead of practicing free shots every spare waking moment, decide to take a break and watch a movie – and if it's a basketball movie, you haven't taken a break! Often taking a break will allow your mind and body to rest and become more effective at your original task. Body builders know that you can't work out constantly; you need to allow your body ample time to rest in order to get the best benefit from your workout.

Here's another example. I am a professional speaker, specializing in helping students motivate themselves to achieve their goals. There are times when business is going gangbusters and I am on fire and in demand, traveling to far-flung places.

Other times, business is slower and, rather than become frustrated and discouraged, I choose to focus on some other dimension of my life. I spend quality time with my wife and friends, indulge my passion for playing Ultimate Frisbee, train in Tae Kwon Do, write, read or even take a nap. The point is that we need to nourish and continually develop different areas of life, and only by devoting appropriate time to them can we do so. The best part is that, once you find what the right balance, all the areas of your life will grow. There will be a ripple effect in development from one area to another. When things are going well with my relationships, I find that business tends to thrive. When business is good, I find I play frisbee more skillfully, and so on.

Optimizing results is about picking which elements of your existence you choose to focus on and putting your heart into maximizing your effectiveness in those areas. As you do this, don't be afraid to change your mind and vary your concentration as you go. At one point, school may be the most important thing to you, but at another it might be your family or your job. Balance means changing things as you evolve while keeping the big picture in mind.

Balance all elements – use fire and water, laughter and tears, seriousness and humor, peanut butter and chocolate. These are the building blocks of life. Life's yings and yangs in the right combination help us create the life we want.

Some of you may be wondering what balance has to do with leadership. The answer is simple; it creates stability. If you are building a house or a skyscraper, you need to start with a solid foundation. Balance is that solid foundation. If you are extreme in any aspect of your well-being, you will be off-centre and more likely to topple over. If all you ever care about is school and every decision and choice ALWAYS has to do with school, you are unstable. You are letting school run your life, instead of school being part of the life you choose to run.

Let me clarify - there is nothing wrong with specializing in one thing. In fact, all successful people do learn to specialize. But even those successful people who are highly specialized, like a doctor who only does one particular type of brain surgery, still have other things that keep them balanced, whether it is family, golf or video games.

When we talk about balance, we start to see there are no universal rules. What worked in one situation may not work in another. We need to learn to be chameleons, adapting to the people and situations around us to give and get the best in each experience we encounter.

Learning balance comes from trial and error. What works for someone else may not work for you. You need to try it and see if it works. You need to fail and make mistakes in order to understand what really works well. Sometimes jumping in and get wet is the best approach, and other times you need to be patient and just dip a toe into the water. There is no ONE right answer: every situation dictates the action.

I remember buying my first computer. At the time, I spent big bucks to get a fancy system loaded with all the bells and whistles. I could have bought the same computer a few months later for much less. So naturally, I kicked myself, cursing my impatience. I could have put that same money to far better use than lining the coffers of some box store.

In retrospect, I now see that I actually did get a pretty good deal at the time. Sure, a better deal came along later, and if I had waited further, I could have gotten a still better deal at an even later date. My point is that there are many opportunities that will come our way, and sometimes it's best not to jump at the first one. Opportunity knocks, but very often it knocks again. But on the flip side, don't spend your entire life waiting for the ultimate opportunity, because it may never come. And even if does, if you've spent all your life waiting, you may decide to wait a little more, in which case you will miss your big chance altogether.

When you have mastered the ability to know when to wait and when to jump, you have mastered balance. Chances are if you are human you will make mistakes along the way – and that's great. Those mistakes form your experience and inform your wisdom.

Balance comes from acquiring wisdom from the mistakes you make along the way.

Here's an analogy for you girls. Pretend that you are going dress shopping for your prom. You try on the first dress - and then you compare each subsequent dress you try on to that first one. You may think, "This one is really nice but too expensive." "I like this one, but it would be really nice if it were in another color." "This one is perfect, but they don't have my size!" … and so on. Now, as long as you keep looking, you can probably always find a better dress - maybe one a little cheaper, perhaps one of slightly better quality. The problem is that if you spend all your time looking for the perfect dress, you could miss the prom!

Don't miss the prom. Use your judgment and experience, and know that sometimes you may have to settle for something less than the grand-perfect-ultimate-opportunity. You can't always give 100% to every club, project, relationship and team; you need to learn your limits, determine the right balance and have a great time at the prom.

While I was finishing my Masters degree in Business Administration (MBA), I went to Denmark to pick up a course to accelerate my program. The course I took was essentially an international case competition, where we were placed in groups with other participants in the program. Each group, comprised of people from different countries, was given a company case-study to examine, and tasked with recommending ways it might improve its business.

My group consisted of a Portuguese, a Hungarian, a Briton and myself (a Canadian). There was much diversity within the group in addition to nationality. Among us, we spoke six languages; there were both genders, an age gap of 27 years between the oldest and youngest and great religious diversity. Nevertheless, we were able to put aside all our differences and work together quite effectively. In fact, our group took first place in the case competition.

This was not because we were smarter or more experienced than any of the other twenty groups; we simply worked better together as a team. We were able to build on our commonalities instead of focusing on our differences and create balance. Often it is a summation of a bunch of small things that make a huge difference. Let me explain using Lego.

A Danish company introduced Lego many years ago and in Billund, Denmark, there is an amusement park called "Legoland." When I decided to go to Denmark, this was definitely on my list of places to visit because...okay, because Lego is cool. As a child, I wanted every piece of Lego in the world. I wanted to build Lego sculptures, Lego cities, and Lego people. Well that's what Legoland is! It has the Statue of Liberty, mini-cities and Darth Vader, all made of Lego. Plus there are thousands of kids, hundreds of cameras and tons of warm Danish hospitality, not to be mistaken for warm Danishes.

What amazed me most about the whole experience was the size and detail of these Lego structures. They did not use any "fancy" Lego pieces when they built Lego-Mount-Rushmore; they used a plan, patience and the same little standard pieces that we all played with as kids. Yet with these small pieces, they were able to create enormous constructions that seemed impossibly complex – one small piece at a time.

Not all the pieces were the same; they varied in size, color and shape. But each served the objective, whether it was to create a building, an alligator, R2D2 or a car. This is what our group did. We used little standard pieces of open-mindedness, acceptance, unity and understanding, and we were able to build a team that was recognized and honored in this grand international setting.

Often we forget that with a plan, patience, and the same little standard pieces of life that we have always had access to, we can build huge creations that seem impossible to others. These small little segments might come in the form of a smile to a co-worker, holding the door for someone at the mall or welcoming a younger student at school. These principles apply to family, work, school, exercise or play.

We have the ability to make any team as successful as we choose. We just need to remember that enough of these small pieces, regardless of their size, color or shape, can make a very large positive difference. The

57

next time you see something that seems impossible, remember that it is just a combination of a plan, patience, the right balance and the same little standard pieces of life that make it possible.

 **LEADERSHIP JOURNAL AND EXERCISES**

1. If you have not completed your Leadership Journal and Exercises from the previous chapter, please do that first.

2. Think of an average school day. Write down all the things you do in that day, and beside each item, write down the average amount of time you spend on each activity. Some things to consider are: school, sleep, homework, socializing, watching TV, work, sports, friends, phone, surfing the web, walking to and from school, volunteer. I recognize that you may not work everyday, but pick an average. So, if you work seven hours a week, that works out to an hour a day.

3. Once you've created that list make another list with the same activities and this time write down the ideal amount of time you would like to spend on each activity.

You may need to add one or two items that you currently are not doing but would like to start. (see the chart below for an example)

You should notice a couple of things. First, it is hard to make it add up to 24 hours. In fact, you might surprise yourself as to how much you are currently trying to do and how you've managed to keep it to 24 hours. Second, if the two columns are not EXACTLY the same, then you do not have the perfect balance you currently want. There is an opportunity to grow here.

Activity	Question 2 (hours) –	Question 3 (hours) – Ideal
School	6	6
Sleep	8	8
Homework	2	1
Socializing	1	1
Watching TV	2	1
Work	0.5	2
Sports	0.5	1
Friends	0.5	1
Phone	1	0.5
Surfing the Web	2	1
Walking to and from	0.5	0.5
Volunteer	0	1
Total	24	24

4. Describe a strategy to make the numbers in Question 2 the same as the numbers in Question 3. In the above example, the goal is to drop homework from two hours a day to one hour a day. In order to do that, I will need a strategy to become more effective when I am doing homework, perhaps a tutor. Write a plan on how you are going make the change from your current to your ideal and have a richer balance in your life.

5. A big key to achieving balance is through reward systems. Sometimes creating balance means pushing ourselves through activities that we normally try to get out of doing. One way to motivate ourselves is to reward ourselves. For example, if normally you hate mowing the lawn, and would rather watch baseball, then make

watching the baseball game your reward for mowing the lawn.

6. What do you consider to be your greatest weaknesses? Do you think these weaknesses are holding you back? If so, what are three ways you can improve the weakness?

7. What do you consider to be your greatest strength? Do you ever take a break from thinking and acting on this strength? What are ten things you can do that will give you a break from obsessing with your strengths?

BELIEF

"Whether you think you can or you can't, you are right."
- Henry Ford

"We don't like their sound, and guitar music is on the way out."
- Decca Recording Co. rejecting the Beatles, 1962.

"Drill for oil? You mean drill into the ground to try and find oil? You're crazy."
- Drillers who Edwin L. Drake tried to enlist to his project to drill for oil in 1859.

"The concept is interesting and well-formed, but in order to earn better than a 'C,' the idea must be feasible."
- A Yale University management professor in response to Fred Smith's paper proposing reliable overnight delivery service. (Smith went on to found Federal Express Corp.)

"But what ... is it good for?"
- Engineer at the Advanced Computing Systems Division of IBM, 1968, commenting on the microchip.

"Who the hell wants to hear actors talk?"
- H.M. Warner, Warner Brothers, 1927.

"If I had thought about it, I wouldn't have done the experiment. The literature was full of examples that said you can't do this."
- Spencer Silver on the work that led to the unique adhesives for 3-M "Post-It" Notepads.

"There is no reason anyone would want a computer in their home."
- Ken Olson, president, chairman and founder of Digital Equipment Corp., 1977.

"This 'telephone' has too many shortcomings to be seriously considered as a means of communication. The device is inherently of no value to us."
- Western Union internal memo, 1876.

"The wireless music box has no imaginable commercial value. Who would pay for a message sent to nobody in particular?"
- David Sarnoff's associates in response to his urgings for investment in the radio in the 1920s.

"Louis Pasteur's theory of germs is ridiculous fiction."
- Pierre Pachet, Professor of Physiology at Toulouse, 1872.

The number one thing that holds people back from being successful is not skills, education, money or opportunity – it is belief. People who become successful believe that they can do it. People who blame everyone and everything else do not believe in their hearts that they deserve to be successful. As a result, they never will. They suffer from what I call 'victimitis.' They feel the world is against them and they will never really be successful. As a result of that thinking, they never truly are.

When I was in high school, a teacher once told me something very interesting. I will paraphrase what he said:

"With all the science known to man, with fax machines and cell phones, with our ability to launch people into space and go to the moon, with all our knowledge, I find it humorous that we still haven't figured out how bumblebees fly. According to the science we currently know, the surface area of the wingspan to the mass of the bumble bee ratio indicates that it is impossible for a bee to fly.

They describe the flight path of a bee by calling them 'extended leaps.' I don't know about you, but I have seen bumblebees … and they fly. I think it's because no one ever told them they couldn't fly. And because they don't know that, they don't let the law of gravity stand in their way of flying.

I believe we humans are a lot like bees. We sometimes won't even try things because we are told they are not possible. But sometimes, without even knowing it, we do the impossible, only because we believe we can. Imagine going through life understanding that the biggest limitation to what you can achieve is your own mindset. That means that if you aren't getting exactly what you want in life, all you have to do is change what you think. You don't have to change your teachers, or parents, or boyfriend or girlfriend. You just have to change your beliefs.

The ability to change obstacles into opportunities is paramount for success. I once read that the invention of the Post-It note was an experiment in which the inventor was trying to make an unbreakable adhesive but failed miserably. But, rather than play victim and be set back by that obstacle, he turned it into an opportunity. That opportunity became a multimillion-dollar business.

Two people in the exact same situation in life will see different things. What you see depends upon your belief. There are people who would attempt to make a super-glue and end up with a Post-It note, and feel that they'd messed up and have a pity party for themselves. But there are others who truly believe they will be successful and look for the chance to convert obstacles into opportunities.

As a teenager, sometimes I would take the bus to school. I only did this when I was too lazy to walk, which was pretty often. The bus drive wasn't too long – only about three traffic lights. No big deal, but one day we managed to hit every single green light. This was odd and it threw off my timing for the entire morning. I arrived at school two minutes early. Invariably, when you are bored, it is best to be bored with others. So I went to the cafeteria where my friends and I engaged in some cards.

Now, I am pretty sure that your school culture is similar to mine. Everyone would hang out in the "cafe" waiting for the day to begin. Some friends of mine were passing time playing penny poker and they invited me to join them. Between the time I sat down and the time the National Anthem started, I won 13 cents. That may sound like small change, but to me it was two and a half sour key candies.

For me, everything in high school could be expressed as a function of sour keys. Those tart candies had a stranglehold on my adolescent life!

The bell rang and I was off to first period, merrily chewing those leathery sour candies. As soon as I walked into the classroom, I remembered I did not want to be there. We'd had a quiz the day before and on the way out of class I was comparing answers with all my friends, and, well, it is usually a bad sign when yours are completely different! Surely I had failed. I got the quiz back. The score was 10 out of 10! It turns out that it was all my friends that had failed! Naturally, I savored the moment by rubbing their faces in my sweet victory. Hey, I never said I was a good friend.

The rest of the day was excellent as well. At lunch, the cafeteria was serving my favorite meal, beef-bean-burrito! I ate up, heeded the call of nature and was off to last period. I believe that 'last period' is Latin for 'most boring class known to mankind.' But there was a substitute teacher who said the sweetest words a teacher can say to a last period class: "Today we will be watching a movie."

The lights went out and so did I. It was perfect timing for my afternoon siesta.

I think I might have slept in a little too long because I almost missed my bus. For consistency reasons, I figure if I'm going to be lazy in the morning and take the bus, I should do the same in the afternoon. Fortunately, my yelling and screaming caught the attention of the bus driver and I made it.

I jumped on the bus and there was only one seat left - right next to this girl I had been dying to meet! I sat down next to her and started "schmoozing it up." "Hey, baby, what's your name? Come here often?" ... you know, really laying on the charm. Things were going great. It turned out she was getting off at the same bus stop as me.

As we were departing the bus, I started thinking to myself, "Today was pretty good." I was having a good hair day. My deodorant was kickin'. I had really put my best foot forward. Unfortunately, right into a pile of dog poop. Literally.

There it was, oozing out the sides of my shoe, and, though horrified, I tried to be subtle and to hide my accident from my new lady friend. "So," I said, "I guess I'll see you tomorrow?" To which she gave me a 'whatever' look and walked away in the opposite direction. I was left to walk home dragging my foot behind me, and to make sure I had rubbed it all off, I even did that moonwalk-like step through the grass.

When I reached my home, my mom was like some mother out of the movies, waiting for me with a tray of milk and cookies, asking, "Hi, Sunjay, how was your day?"

"TERRIBLE!" I replied, "It was the worst day ev…"

I stopped myself there and rethought my response. "Pretty good," I said.

My day hadn't been terrible at all. In fact, it was a pretty good day. I won 13 cents, two and a half sour keys, got ten out of ten on the quiz, ate a beef bean burrito, took a nap, and met a girl. What was I doing? I was focusing on the one crappy moment. No pun intended.

When I was in University, I learnt that psychologists have a term for this. They call it a negativity bias. As humans, we are often biased to remember the negative things more than the positive things in life. It is understandable that if your beliefs are negative, your attitudes are negative. What happens in your life stems from your beliefs; whether passing a test or hitting a homerun, if you don't believe you can do it, you won't.

What's Red?

One day, hanging out with friends, one of them said she had a test to try on all of us. So we listened to her instructions.

"Look around you and find all the things around you that are red," she said and gave us a minute to look around.

"Good," she said, "Now that you have done that, close your eyes."

Once all of us had closed our eyes she asked, "How many things around you are *blue*?"

I think that I was able to name about two items that were blue. Once I opened my eyes I instantly found 12 more blue things. It wasn't really fair. She tricked us. I wasn't looking for blue things; all of my attention was on things that were red. If she had asked me about the red items, I could have easily rhymed off eight. Why did she ask about blue? I was completely ignoring all the other colors.

Perception is a very powerful tool. We have the power and ability to block out things that are right in front of us. On the flipside, we can see only things that we want to see. A perfect example of this is a man in a desert who sees a mirage of water in the middle of nowhere.

Why does he see the water? Because he wants to. Athletes have been using this technique for years. Many athletes practice going through competition in their head. They see, hear, taste, touch and smell victory in their minds first. Once that belief is engrained, they go and make it reality on the field, court or ring. I have always based my life on the simple principle that what you believe you will become. Here's an example.

In third grade, I wasn't the most athletic kid. In fact, people would often pick a gym bag over me when choosing sports teams. I used to dream about being more athletic. So I selected those around me who were good athletes to serve as role models. I noticed that a lot of the older athletes like high school students – and boy, were they old - like 12 or 13 easy -  would wear tensor bands or braces around their knees. So in my third-grade wisdom, I somehow concluded that being athletic meant that you had to wear tensor bands and therefore have knee problems. My belief system now included the notion that to be athletic you need to have bum knees. I was focusing on all the red things around me. I became one-track-minded. I used to wish that I would have to wear tensor bands or knee braces so that I, too, could be athletic. Well, be careful what you wish for because it just might come true.

By the time I was in tenth grade, my knees were totally messed up. At the time, I was training in Tae Kwon Do and my knees were so damaged that my doctor instructed me to quit martial arts because my knees couldn't take it. I got exactly what I wanted. The problem was that what I thought I wanted, I didn't really want.

We really need to be aware of how our beliefs shape our lives. On the plus side, after taking several years off of martial arts and really wanting to get back into it, my belief system changed. I believed despite having damaged knees, I could still somehow make it work. A few years later I discovered custom orthotics and that made all the difference in the world. I was able to train again without the pain. It's amazing how when you truly believe something, the universe makes it possible for you to achieve it.

It was the same as when my friend asked me to spot all the red things around me. I was so focused on one single result that I missed a bunch of other things around me. What I should have been doing was concentrating on becoming  more athletic and focusing on the other colors around me. Keep an open mind, learn to look for the colors around you and enjoy the rainbow of choice.

When you believe, you achieve.

 **LEADERSHIP JOURNAL AND EXERCISES**

1. If you have not completed your Leadership Journal and Exercises from the previous chapter, please do that first.

2. What are some of the philosophies that you base your life on that not everyone would agree with? For example, nice guys finish last or success is a matter of luck, etc.

3. Make a list of all the people you know who have been successful without having all the opportunities that you have.

4. Do you truly believe with all your mind and heart that you have all the abilities and opportunities to be as successful as you would like? Explain.

5. If you knew you could not fail, what would you try? If you believe that failure is not getting the outcome you wanted, then people will constantly fail. However, if you choose to define failure as learning from your experience, there is no failure. You can try anything you want and know that you won't fail. You may not get the outcome you wanted but you can learn from that experience and move on. Why are you waiting?

   Has someone ever made you feel that you weren't good enough? That's unfortunate if they did, but what is even more unfortunate is you chose to believe them. When you believe you persevere. The opening of this chapter provided many examples from history where people were ridiculed for challenging the status quo. There will always be non-believers. You will always face resistance. That is why you need to believe in yourself, so even in times of others doubting you, you will move on. Add three quotes to this list from people in your past that have rejected you.

But you believe that you will be successful regardless of what they've said. For example, I might write:

"Sunjay is too quiet and shy to ever have a job that would involve interacting with people on a daily basis."

Mrs. Ancaster, Sunjay's fifth grade teacher.

(Hah Mrs. Ancaster. Hah!)

6. To change your belief system you just need to change your self-talk. By repeating to yourself what you want to believe, you will become. For example, everyday say to yourself, "I am successful at all that I do and constantly help those around me to achieve their dreams." This will become part of your beliefs and you will start living according to this.

Write your daily mantra and say it to yourself as many times as you can during all idle times of the day (falling asleep, waiting in line, just waking up, etc).

BEHAVIOR

"Behavior is a mirror in which every one displays his own image."

■ **Johann Wolfgang von Goethe**

So far, in the "B" section of this book, we have talked about Balance and Belief, as both produce the third "B" dictate your success. The good news is that those behaviors do not have to be extreme.

I looked up the definition for behavior:

"The action or reaction of something (as a machine or substance) under specified circumstances."

I think that definition is perfect. How do you act or react to things around you? Are you a stress-monger? Do you lose your temper quickly? Do you stick to the plan? Are you a team player? Do you sit  on the couch rocking back and forth in the fetal position eating boxes of chocolates when things don't go your way? A true test to determine your behavior is how you act if no-one is around and you think nobody is watching. Are you more likely to litter if you think you can get away with it? When it comes to behavior, a leader is the same person in private as in public. Leadership is an internal quality or drive that is not changed by the number of people around. What is right for a true leader in front of a group of 10,000 is still right for the leader when he or she is alone.

I remember buying my first new car - well, new to me. Okay, so it was a used car. That meant that for several weeks leading up to the purchase, I had had the distinct

 pleasure of dealing with used car salesmen. Not to be stereotypical, but some of them were stereotypical used car salesmen – slick and slimy, and those were just their good points. I was made promises of great value, status, coolness and women, if only I would buy a particular car. As far as I know, this is a fairly common practice. Salesmen know that we tend to associate internal attributes of an individual with his or her external material possessions; we think that the clothes or the car or the house make the person. The reality is none of that matters.

We definitely live in a very materialistic society and some people will 'buy' right into that. Peers will try to convince you that having certain clothes or buying the latest gizmo will make you a better person. Again, the reality is that none of that matters. I have seen elementary school kids, as well as high school students and beyond, be particularly mean to people because they were different. I have actually witnessed, on more than one occasion, people being called 'losers' for the ring on their cell phone or for liking a particular song. Does this really make or break us in the coolness department? One more time: the reality is that none of that matters.

What does matter is what **you** think of **you** and how **you** feel about **you**. If you take away all the iPods and car stereos, make-up and clothes, we are all people - a bunch of naked people standing around with nothing but what is inside us. What makes or breaks a person is not what music he/she listens to, what cell phone ring he/she uses or what car he/she drives. What really matters is the person on the inside. Some of the quietest people at my school were some of the people that got picked on the most. They were also, after I got to know them, some of the coolest, funniest and most talented people around.

As student leaders in your school, I urge you to set an example and try to make everyone in your school feel welcome. Say hi to everyone you know and even the people you don't. When people are getting picked on, don't perpetuate the process. Try changing the subject or standing up for the individual, especially if you know what is being said is not true. You behaviors, your actions and reactions to circumstances, will shape your leadership style. Make your school, your community and your world a place where being different is not a bad thing. Embrace your individuality and help others do the same one little step at a time.

In fact, simple, modest, easy, consistent steps along the way often will get you to your finish line much more quickly and consistently than extravagant, short-lived ones. Small changes in behavior over a long period of time will yield better results than large changes in behavior over short periods of time.

Let me try to explain this concept with money and something called compound interest. Compound interest is one of the simplest yet most effective ways that the rich become rich and richer. The basic premise of this is: Why work for money when money can work for you?

Just as a bank can make money by loaning money – you and I, as investors, can do the same thing. The longer time we have money, the more money we can make; and the higher the interest rate we can get, the more money we make.

That's how you make money work for you. You don't have to do anything other than loan your money out. Let the money work. You invest it, or loan it to companies or banks so that you get interest for it.

The best part of investing is that, when you invest wisely enough and long enough, the interest you earn will earn interest, too. When your interest starts to earn interest, that's called compound interest.

So let's use an example. Say you decide you are going to start saving some money. Nothing grandiose, just $2 a day. You figure you can easily do that and your plan is to save that money for one year. However, for the last month of the year, you decide to change your behavior, work really hard and save $10 each day in that month.

Let's calculate how much money you will have at the end of the month:
$2/day x 335 days + $10/day x 30 days = $970.

That is an example of making a large change over a small period of time. At the end of the year you are sitting pretty with $970. That's pretty impressive. However, let's look at what happens when you make small changes over a large period of time. We will assume that you start off saving $2 per day; however, each day, you save an extra 1% over the day before. So the first day you save $2.00, the second day you save $2.00 plus 1% which is $2.02, the third day you save $2.02 plus 1% which is $2.0402 – which you round to $2.04.

Guess how much money you would have saved at the end of the year? It would be worth $7356.69. That is more than seven times more money than saving the other way. Now if you really want to see the power of making small changes over a long period of time, let's examine these examples over five years.

After five years of saving $2 per day and one month a year saving $10 per day, you would have a grand total of $4850.00 saved. Using small changes over a long period of time and increasing your saving efforts by 1% per day – after 5 years you would have saved, just over $15.4 billion. The exact number looks like this: $15,400,582,350.11. Pretty impressive, eh? Now, you could do some serious shopping with that kind of cash.

Keep in mind that this doesn't only work for money, it works for everything. If you choose to do an extra push-up, or homework question or give an extra hug, those small actions and behavior changes over a large period of time can make a very big difference.

If you constantly improve just a bit, as time goes by, you will see significant improvement.

To be great, you do not have to do anything dramatic, you just have to make small changes over a large period of time and give yourself the opportunity to let your greatness, which is in all of us, ooze out.

Increasing and improving by only 1% from the previous day is not a large task. In fact, over a short amount of time you would barely even notice it. However, over time it makes a HUGE difference. When it comes to altering behaviors, look to make small changes over a large period of time rather than large changes of a short period of time.

What if you could improve your behaviors, your thoughts, your beliefs and your actions by just 1% per day? It's just a small change – and over time it can make a huge difference. Your behavior is how you act or react in circumstances. When things don't work out your way, do you look for an out and start to pout? Or do you think how that experience has served you and stretch yourself to be 1% better?

If you haven't been convinced that little things add up, let me use this example. Experts say that you should spend a minimum of three minutes brushing your teeth and you should brush your teeth a minimum of three times a day. Now, assume that the average life span is 80 years – and you spend that nine minutes a day brushing your teeth. The average person spends 182.5 days of his life brushing his teeth! WOW! Little things add up quick – especially if you are patient.

You don't run a marathon the first day out. Instead you just start off by running the width of a football field, then grow that to the length of the field, then to around the block ... and soon you will be running farther that you ever thought possible. You can run the marathon, but don't feel you have to do it in one day. As a friend of mine's piano teacher says, "how do you eat an elephant? One bite at a time."

If you think you are watching too much TV and you want to change that behavior, you don't need to stop watching TV tomorrow. Watch five minutes less each day. I would suggest missing the first 5 minutes of a show – that way you still get to know what happens at the end.

Your behavior is the same way. You may find that you do not always behave the way you want. Perhaps you get frustrated or angered easily – don't worry, you can very easily change your actions and reactions to whatever you want them to be. Don't feel the need to make the changes all at once – just make small changes over a long period of time. You'd be surprised how quickly the time will actually pass when you see the results come in. Over time, you will always get to your finish line as long as your behaviors and actions are in line with one another.

LEADERSHIP JOURNAL AND EXERCISES

1. If you have not completed your Leadership Journal and Exercises from the previous chapter, please do that first.

2. Behaviors form habits. Write down ten good habits that you think you have. Then write down ten good habits that you wish you did have. What behaviors can you change to start forming these habits?

3. Write down ten bad habits that you think you have. What behaviors can you change to reduce or eliminate these habits?

4. The difference between good and great is small things done over time. What can you do to make yourself 1% better each day? Consider all areas of your life from school to athletics, from work to social.

5. What types of behaviors surround you? Think about the actions of your friends and family that influence you? Which of these behaviors do you choose to emulate? Which of these behaviors do you choose to avoid? Remember, unless you make a conscious effort to control the behaviors around you, they will control you. Learn to accept and reject behaviors.

6. What attributes of your personality have you been shy about exposing? What type of person are you when you are by yourself? Write a list of three things that are unique about you that you are

afraid to share with others. For each of those three things, come up with ten reasons why you should be proud to share that attribute.

7. When interacting with others, keep in mind that the behaviors a person demonstrates are often different from who that person really is. If someone is driving really slow in front of you, rather than get upset with the person, get upset with the behavior.

Be nice to people but tough on behaviors that challenge you. Pick a behavior of someone that has been driving you nuts for a long time and approach that person to discuss the behavior. Make sure you distinguish between the person and the behavior. A sentence that might help to do this is: "When you do this (insert behavior, i.e. chew your toe nails), it drives me nuts" as opposed to "You are such an idiot for chewing your toe nails." One statement attacks the behavior and the other attack the person. Only attack the behavior.

COMMITMENT

"There is no poverty that can overtake diligence."
■ **Japanese proverb**

As long as I can remember, I've always believed the cliché, "Where there's a will there's a way." When a group or individual is totally committed to making something happen – it happens. That can be both a good thing and a bad thing.

A leader is a person who can clearly define his or her purpose and commit to that purpose with such conviction that it inspires others to do the same.

We have seen examples of this throughout history, from leaders like Mother Theresa, Martin Luther King Jr. and Gandhi.

All three of them are fantastic examples of committed individuals. They were able to walk down a path that was not always that popular and in doing so inspire millions of others to do the same. Commitment on its own is not a good or bad thing; it is a tool, just like fire. It can be harnessed and used for benefit or it can be mishandled and put to ill use.

Just as with the other ABCs we've addressed, commitment is an internal quality. You don't fake commitment – you own it.

Many years ago, I read a story about Gandhi. Apparently, a lady brought her son to see him and explained, "My son eats too much sugar. Tell him he eats too much sugar. I've tried to tell him but he will not listen to me. Hopefully he'll listen to you."

"Come back in two weeks," he told the mother and child.

Two weeks later, the mother and child returned with the same plea, "Tell him he eats too much sugar."

Gandhi grabbed the kid, looked him straight in the eye and said, "You eat too much sugar. It's not good for you. Stop it." The mother was very thankful, but couldn't resist asking, "Why didn't you tell him that two weeks ago when we were here?"

He smiled and responded, "Two weeks ago, I ate too much sugar."

Commitment comes from within. The only way you truly commit to something is when your inner self buys into the action. You cannot fake commitment. Yes, there are people who will pretend to buy into something, but sooner or later they will find out that they are being dishonest to themselves and they will right their path.

Gandhi knew that hypocritical advice doesn't resonate and that only counsel which is inwardly and outwardly congruent has value. Gandhi would also say that a man cannot do "right" in one area of his life while knowingly doing wrong in another. Your commitment needs to be congruent internally and externally.

I meet a surprising number of students every year of whom I ask the question, "What do you want to do with life beyond school?" It surprises me how many of their responses start off, "My parents want me to be ..."

I didn't ask what your parents want you to do, I tell them, I was asking what *you* want to do. The problem with buying into someone else's vision is  that, if you are not totally committed to it, it is unstable. You may do something for other people just to please them, but if it doesn't sit right with who you are, it will eventually lead you to feel depressed, frustrated or angry. This is often where mid-life crisis come from.

People have been buying into others' visions for how they should be living their lives. Then at some point, they break and say they've had enough. Then they choose to make major life changes that reflect their true desires and they start living more consistently with who they truly are. The person who chases two rabbits often ends up with none. I heard Gill Grison say that in an episode of CSI.

I used to be indecisive. Now, I'm just not sure!

Decision is the key to commitment. Sometimes it is hard to stick to a decision. When I was younger, my parents would tell me this story:

Once upon a time, there was a poor boy who was very hungry. He was walking through the market when he decided he was going to steal something to eat, so as soon as the storekeeper looked away, the boy grabbed the closest piece of food that he could. It turned out to be an onion. He left the store and started eating the onion. Unfortunately, it was not a clean getaway for the boy, because the storekeeper saw him and followed him out of the store.

"You dare steal from me? Do you know what the consequences of stealing are?" shouted the storekeeper.

"I'm sorry," cried the boy, "It's just that I am very hungry and poor."

"No one is poor enough to steal an onion," insisted the storekeeper.

"I am," replied the boy.

"Well, then, if you are willing to eat onions, I can make you a deal. I will not report you to the police. However, in return, you have two choices. One, you can eat twenty-five whole onions or two, you can dig a well that is twenty-five feet deep."

 The boy was delighted at the thought of twenty-five free onions so he chose that option and started eating. One, two, three, four onions he ate. By the fifth, his mouth was starting to burn, by the sixth his eyes were streaming and he barely finished the seventh. He asked the storekeeper if he could change his mind and when the storekeeper agreed, the boy started to dig.

One, two, three, four feet deep, he dug the well. This was very hard work; by the fifth foot his back was aching, by the sixth his hands were aching, and he barely dug the seventh. He begged the storekeeper to allow him to switch back to eating the onions. The storekeeper agreed and the boy continued from where he left off.

Eight, nine ... he didn't remember eating the onions being this difficult; he was barely able to finish the tenth; he decided that digging the well was definitely easier than eating the onions. So once again he switched, and again he had problems with the digging. The sun was too hot, he was very thirsty, and ... eating those onions wasn't so bad after all.

He switched, and switched again. He switched back and he switched forth, he switched so many times that he lost count sometimes. But in the end, he did it - he finally ate the twenty-five onions. He was free to go, and as he left, the storekeeper thanked him for digging a twenty-five-foot well.

The moral of the story is to commit to your plan and follow it. In the end, it can save you a lot of time and effort.

When you are truly committed to something, you do not easily get diverted from your goal. You will have setbacks, but you will just change your course of action and continue to pursue that goal. One time, as I was returning home from Chicago, I looked out the airplane window at clouds so thick that I couldn't even see the wing of the plane. Even when the plane dipped below the clouds, the visibility didn't improve much because it was an extremely foggy night.

The pilots in the cockpit were just as sightless as the rest of us on the plane, yet they still knew where they were going and were committed to getting the passengers to their destination. The passengers on the plane did not panic. We did not get worried and start  freaking out, running up in down the aisles in frantic disarray. We just sat calmly as if everything were under control. And rightfully so, because indeed it was.

Now, if this situation had been me and a bunch of my buddies in a car where the driver couldn't see three feet in front of him, there would definitely be need for alarm. The smart thing to do would have been to pull over and wait until the weather improved.

Why are these circumstances different? Well, for one thing, it is very difficult to pull over an airplane at 32,000 feet until the weather passes.

More importantly, the pilots have a support team that is just as committed as they are to getting the plane to its final destination. An effective team will help you and support you to stay committed.

It's really quite simple. Before a flight takes off, the crew assembles with a common goal, in this case to safely bring the plane from Chicago to Toronto. The grounds crew, the people in the tower, and the attendants and pilots on the plane are all aware of this goal and are committed to it. If any member of the team loses sight of the goal, the rest of the team is there to help that member back on track. Even though the pilots may have lost physical view of where they are heading, they still had the trust and confidence of the rest of their team to guide them to their destination.

In the case of my friends and I joy-riding in bad weather, we don't have the luxury of a mission control tower. We are independent and the only ones aware of our final destination.

In student leadership, there are many control towers that will help you when you need it. You just have to learn to spot them and not be afraid to utilize them. Staff advisors, parents, teachers and friends can all help. Can you recall an incident where you were bummed out and the encouraging words of a friend helped you out of the dump? You can try to tackle your problems on your own and you might even have some success. But every so often, the weather gets so bad that you have to pull over and let it clear.

If you make use of your support team, you will have more successes and less need to pull over and watch life. Instead, you could be driving in the fast lane or soaring through the clouds.

Someone once told me an amazing stat – an airplane is off course 97% of the time! That means that pilots are constantly redirecting and correcting the flight path to compensate for things like wind patterns and air turbulence. When you are committed to making something happen, even if you get side-tracked you will right your course. Commitment helps you see more opportunities than obstacles. The stronger your commitment is to your goal, the easier it is to stick to it when you are going through turbulence or rough times.

 **LEADERSHIP JOURNAL AND EXERCISES**

1. If you have not completed your Leadership Journal and Exercises from the previous chapter, please do that first.

2. Make a list of three things that you can commit to start doing today and will commit to do everyday for the next 28 days. Now do it!

3. Who is your control tower? Who are the people in your life that support you and guide you when you hit bad weather? How do you show that you are grateful for what they do for you?

4. Who are you a control tower for? Are you clear on what is important to these individuals so that you can help them stay committed to what is most important to them? Have a conversation about what is most important to them. This way you can help guide them better. A control tower is always much more effective when they know the final destination.

5. What is your final destination? Write a mission statement for your life. A mission statement gives you an overall purpose for your life. When you write your mission it is more of a destination and less about a process.

   For example, to be a teacher or doctor are not missions because they are processes of how to do something else. An example of a mission may be "to use my talents to help others grow" or "teach the world" or "make the world I encounter a better place because I have come in to it." Can you see how being a teacher or doctor can help facilitate all three of those missions? A mission is a destination, not a process.

6. Now that your mission is written, what does your path to achieve it look like (this is about process)? Are you going to achieve this mission by being a mechanic or a big brother or an aesthetician? Write down milestone goals that need to happen in order for you to achieve this.

   - For example, if your desired path is a mechanic:
     i. you need to get certified as a mechanic
     ii. in order to do that you need to go to mechanic school
     iii. in order to do that you need certain criteria to get into the school

7. Once you have a mission, a path and milestone goals written, go buy some poster paper, and in larger-than-life font put them on the poster board. Then, place the poster board in your room so every time you walk in or out of your room it helps you refocus and stay committed to your mission.

8. For the next week, when you agree to do something, commit 100%. That means go early, leave late and when you are there do your best to be both mentally and physically present. Give all your head and heart in every action you take and you will find it is more fulfilling.

CHANGE

"Be the change you want to see in the world."

■ **Gandhi**

It has been said that the only constant in life is change itself. No matter who you are or what you do, changes will happen. Some will be perceived as positive  and others, not so much. The true test of a leader is how he or she deals with things when they aren't going according to plan.

It is certainly easy to be positive and upbeat when everything is going according to plan. But what happens when things change and the reality you had counted on has been obliterated? How you behave in that situation will go a long way in determining how you lead. Do you become quiet? Stressed? Calm? Annoyed? Resourceful? Excited?

Do not fear change. Change is not good or bad, it's only constant. How you *perceive* change may be positive or negative.

So if it is all about your perception, why not choose to see it as a good thing? Chances are if a change is occurring in your life and you are upset with it, there are probably a bunch of other people who are very happy with that change. Try doing this – think of something that has changed in your life that has made you upset.

Now change your perspective and see how that change can be perceived by someone else as a good thing. Better yet, consider how that change can be perceived by you as a good thing. For example, my girlfriend dumping me can be perceived as bad. But with that situation comes, "perhaps we were not a good fit and it's a good thing we ended the relationship now," or "great, I am available again!!"

If change is neutral and only our perception dictates whether we think it is good or bad, and since we have complete control of our perception, why not always choose to see change as a good thing? Leaders recognize that they have the power to do this.

A core element of leadership is to understand that we cannot change people and we have very little control over most situations. The only thing that we have complete control over is ourselves. We choose how we carry ourselves and how we act and react to every situation we find ourselves in. Leaders recognize that change is an internal action that no-one can do for us.

During the summer after my first year of university, my parents moved from the house that I had grown up in to a condominium. The move made a lot of sense; my parents did not need an entire house and besides, my dad worked close to their new condo. It seemed to be the practical thing to do.

However, there was one very important thing that my parents forgot to account for: my feelings. Hello? This was *my* house, too! This is where I grew up. This was the house in which I had my first co-ed sleepover, where I had my first pet, the first place I kissed a girl. There was a spot on my bedroom wall where I'd tracked my growth over several years. I got my first cavity, I broke my thumb, I shaved my head ... all in that house. And here were my parents ready to sell *my* house! Some nerve!

I was very determined not to let it go – I wasn't ready to accept the change. I tried negotiations, begging, threatening ... I even offered to buy the house! University and College students, who can barely afford PB&J sandwiches, will relate to how funny this is– generally speaking when you suck stains out of a table cloth and call it dinner, you typically do NOT have thousands of dollars lying around to purchase a house. Nothing seemed to work; they were bound and determined to sell my beloved home.

Fine! If that was going to be their attitude, then I would just have to buy the house back from the people who were going to buy the house from my parents, once I graduated from school and become independently wealthy, of course.

As time went on though, I came to realize that owning the house was not what kept the memories alive. What goes on in my head is what makes them precious. And what I *choose* to remember is what my memories are. Rather than pouting and being upset about losing the house, I had the ability to *decide* to make it a positive turn of events. Those stored memories are what have helped shape me into the person I am today. If I focus on how great they were, they will help make me great.

I choose to focus on how great they were. Those experiences are a direct factor of the person I have developed into. I am extremely grateful for them, regardless of whether or not my parents own that house on 5417 Randolph Crescent.

 In high school, I remember when graduation time rolled around; there was a core group of people who felt extremely excited about graduating high school, who couldn't wait for the next chapter of life to begin. On the flip side were people who were very upset to be leaving their home of four years. These people were in the same school, so why were their experiences so different? It reminded me of how my parents and I viewed moving from the house. They were ready to move on and initially I was not. There wasn't any one *right* way to feel. Each group had its own reasons for feeling the way it did. We can't live in the past forever, though - sometimes we have to say, "Hey, this chapter of my life is over and it is time to move forward."

Change is inevitable.

I eventually learned that. Coming to grips with the fact that it was time to move on wasn't easy, but I accepted it. I no longer have a desire to buy the house but I sure do miss it. So every now and then, when I am feeling nostalgic, I will drive by and remember the good times I had while living there. There is nothing wrong with change; in fact, change is obviously what leads to some of the greatest innovations and developments. We should welcome the challenges that accompany change and that will help us to move to our most desired places.

Don't fear change, embrace it. Once I bought some new underwear. Well, more than once, that's gross. It was twice! I went to put my new drawers into my dresser...well, drawer. I found that they didn't all fit in it anymore. So I did some underwear evaluation.

First on the chopping block was an old pair of bikini briefs from 1991 that I can't believe I still had kicking around. Guys bond deeply with their underwear. Just try to get an old pair away from us. It's one of the many deeply peculiar guy mysteries that are, much like and X-File, perhaps better left unsolved! They were one of the first pairs to go. I looked at a pair of boxers that had cannonball-sized holes. I was reluctant to get rid of them because when I first got these boxers, they were my favorites. They were a gift, a girlfriend of mine had made them for me for Christmas. They had flying pigs on them and they fit so well. These were one of those pair of good-luck-gitches.
You know, the kind that you would wear on a date, or an interview, or those that you would save so that you could write your calculus final in them. They were awesome.

The key word here is "were." In their prime, the flying pig boxers were a fabulous garment, crème de la crème. But the more I thought about it, the more I realized that the flying pigs were no longer good-luck gitches. They didn't fit like they used to, the elastic was shot and material was much thinner from all the washes. Through time, heartbreakingly, they had changed. Now they were an old raggedy piece of cloth. And the sad reality is at some point, this is going to happen to my new underwear. They will eventually turn into old junky fabric. Then I will find some new hotshot underwear to replace them.

You are probably sitting there saying to yourself, "I think that I now know a little too much about Sunjay's underwear. Heck, if he wore bikini briefs in 1991, how can I take him seriously? And what is his point, anyway?"

Underwear will come and go. The only constant in your life is you. Wherever you go, that's where you'll be. Things around you will constantly change and it's up to you whether you live in the past or make adjustments for the future.

The next time you are involved with an election, whether of your school student council or the federal leadership, keep in mind that you get to make the same choice. You have the power to be involved with a change that is going to occur.

You can reminisce about the good old times with the old council or the incumbent government and never realize how great the new people are. Or, you can look at the strengths of the newly-elected council and see how they are going to make a great team next year. The choice is yours.

My new underwear doesn't fit me better or worse than my old underwear at its prime. It fits differently; in some ways better and in some ways not. I choose to concentrate on how it's better.

That's the key to change. Change is not good or bad, but is merely how you choose to perceive it. Since you are in control of your perception, choose to see change as a good thing.

LEADERSHiP JOURNAL AND EXERCiSES

1. If you have not completed your Leadership Journal and Exercises from the previous chapter, please do that first.

2. What things in your life have you been thinking about changing but have been too scared or lazy to change? If you implemented those changes, what is the worst thing that could happen? What is the best thing that could happen?

3. Take a trial run. Take the list from Question 2, try implementing those changes for 28 days and see what happens. After 28 days, if you don't like the results revert back to the old way.

4. What are some rewards that you can give yourself for initiating and executing one change? More often than not, the biggest fear people have about change IS the fear, not the change itself. If you give yourself a big enough reason to make the change you will change. If you can alter your understanding so that you see how making the change does more good for you than staying your current course, you will make the change. Make a list of rewards that get you excited and then use them to initiate changes in your life.

5. The most effective way to change people around you is to change yourself and set an example of the change you want to see in others. What are some of the things you want others around you to change?

What changes will you make in your behavior and actions to model that change for others?

6. Make a list of ten changes that have happened to you in the past year. Beside each write down whether it was a good or a bad change. In doing this exercise, you may find that things that initially seemed bad turned out to be good, or things that initially seemed good turned out to be bad.

7. For each item on the list that you've perceived to be good, make a list of five other people who would find this bad.

8. For each item you perceived as bad in the above question, make a list of five people that would find this good. Remember change is not good or bad, only our perceptions are.

9. For the next week, do everything differently. Completely change all your patterns in life. For example when you shower, if you normally shampoo before you soap, then for the next week soap before you shampoo. If you normally walk a certain route to school, change it. Try using the mouse with your left hand rather than your right hand for a week.

    You will find that it is awkward at first – but by the end of the week, it will be no big deal. Most change is like that, once you actually do it, it's no big deal.

CHARACTER

"I want to be unique … just like all my friends."
■ **As seen on a T-shirt**

Character is the set of values that determines who you are, and it is the basis of all your actions and reactions. You can shape your character or it can be shaped for you.

Character is who you are on the inside. And like it or not, that character will constantly come through in almost every action we take.

Have you ever met someone, shook his or her hand and immediately got the "heebie-jeebies?" Or, just the opposite, instantly felt him or her to be very warm and trustworthy? That happens because he is showing his true character, you happened to catch a glimpse of who they are and either it resonated with you and made you feel comfortable or it was not consistent with your own character and you were turned off.

 If you have a garden in your backyard and you don't tend to it, very quickly it will fill with dandelions and weeds. However, if you make a conscious effort to grow specific plants, flowers or vegetables you can, provided you nurture that garden. If you put time, energy, attention and thought into growing a beautiful garden, you will reap the benefits of a harvest, whether it be food or flowers. The only way you grow a weedless, healthy garden is to put in the effort to do so. It doesn't happen by chance.

The same thing is true of your character and mind. If you don't care what grows in the garden of your mind, then anything will take root there. If you happen to like dandelions and weeds, then you'll be content with your harvest. However, if you don't like those plants, then you feel discontent. The best way to assure that you grow the plants you want is to select them carefully, feed them, water them and fertilize them.

A student who has decided not to smoke will not be tempted if he or she is offered a cigarette. He or she will say no thanks, that's gross and be done with it. That's because that individual has planted a no-smoking character plant in the garden of his or her mind. However, if a student who has never thought about smoking is offered a cigarette, he or she might say yes or no. That is a wild seedling that was blown there by the breeze, influenced by external factors like wind direction, climate, weather and a host of other things.

Intuition

We are constantly bombarded by society's messages in the media – TV, radio, newspapers, magazines, the Internet, movies, etc. If we haven't thought through important decisions about who we are and what actions are consistent with our character, we are likely to buy into others' ideas. These ideas are ones that we might not have embraced, had we taken the time to think them through. Who you are on the inside will be revealed in everything you do. The good news is that you have complete control of who you are within.

 Science has shown us, with things like fingerprints and DNA, that whenever you touch something, you leave your mark on it. In fact, no two items in the universe can come in contact with one another and not have an impact on each other. Your character determines that impact. I believe as science evolves, there will be more ways of measuring these impacts which I call character signatures.

Intuition is a word we use to describe people who are very good at spotting other people's character signatures. Let me explain it this way. Everything that we do, from the way we drive to how we close or slam a door to the way we hold our posture, is unique from individual to individual.
Intuitive people have a sense, based on observations, about the true character of each individual.

Viva Las Vegas

I remember my first trip to Las Vegas. One of my very good friends, Victor, was doing a work placement in Utah for the summer, so we figured that it would be a great idea to meet in Vegas for a weekend and donate our fair share of money to the Casinos. Neither of us had ever been there before so we were both pretty excited. We'd seen Vegas on TV and in the movies, and we were looking forward to the glitz and the glamour.

When we got there, we certainly were not disappointed. It was one gigantic spectacle! There were lights and shows, huge buildings, actors and dancers, lions and tigers (and bears, oh my!). It was crazy! The hotels competed with one another, each trying to out-do its neighbor. One hotel had a waterfall that turned into a volcano with smoke and fire. Up the street there was a new hotel that spent $100 million on plants for its landscape. I don't think that there exist more manmade "wonders of nature" in such a small area anywhere else in the world.

At the beginning, we found the scenery overwhelming. It was amazing that people could build such an empire in a desert. That's right, a desert! A desert is a challenging place that people trek across if they have to and if they are lucky, they survive, with only mild dehydration or sunstroke. In Vegas, the challenge people undergo is to trudge from air-conditioned building to air-conditioned building, and if they are lucky, they survive with only mild over-exposure to Elvis.

About the second day into the trip, Victor commented on how everything was so artificial. The only animals around were caged for exhibition. That's when I started to notice how fake everything was. It occurred to me that I hadn't seen or heard a single bird since I'd been there. The casinos had no windows or clocks. There was no natural vegetation. Everything was designed and deliberate; from the planter next to me to the fake waterfall next door. It was eerie.

Don't get me wrong. I am not being a "half-empty" guy. What I am saying is that you can fancy up a desert all you want, but it is still going to be a desert. The character of Las Vegas is that it is just that, a desert. Let me emphasize, there is nothing wrong with being a desert in the first place. How many times have we met someone who tried to be someone he or she was not? Perhaps they were wearing certain clothes to fit in, or doing things they would normally not do, or saying things to impress others. My advice is, stop it. Why? Well, when things don't make sense, people will eventually catch on. In Vegas, at first, I was really impressed.

But, the more I experienced Vegas, the more I realized that things weren't right. If you are a desert, be the best desert that you can be. However, here's the best part: unlike a real desert, people have choice. If you are a desert and you don't want to be one – you don't have to be! If there are certain things about yourself that you want to change, YOU have the ability to change them. Change them within you - don't superficially throw on the latest fashion, reach for your smokes or chug that beer - it doesn't fix things, it only makes them worse.

I am not condemning wearing nice clothes – I love nice clothes. What I am suggesting is that if you don't feel good about yourself, nice clothes will not fix the problem. You need to correct your self-esteem internally and then that will reflect externally. You need to identify and celebrate the magnificent being that you are. If you truly enjoy the fashions, then by all means wear them. Do it for you, not for others. Do it because you enjoy it, not because you think it will "fix" you. If you want to make a change, go within you and change from the inside out, not the outside in.

If you feel like you don't fit in and you go and buy an expensive car to try to fit in better, you still won't fit in. Now you'll be someone with an expensive car and a large debt that still doesn't fit in.

If you want to fit in, recognize that you are a wonderful person with great value to offer and surround yourself with people who appreciate you for you. Change is an internal process that shows up externally – not the other way around.

Sure, Vegas can spend another $2 billion and build another hotel, but Vegas will always be a desert. I think Vegas is a great success story. It is a great example of being the best desert it  can be. Remember, as people, we have the choice to make any change we want. If we think we are a desert, in the landscape of our minds we have the ability to add lakes, streams and even an ocean, if we choose. First, figure out if you are a polar ice cap or a rainforest, a desert, a mountain, or a marsh. Celebrate what you are happy with, change what you don't like from the inside out, be proud of the final product and use it to your advantage to be the best leader you can be.

LEADERSHIP JOURNAL AND EXERCISES

1. If you have not completed your Leadership Journal and Exercises from the previous chapter, please do that first.

2. Who are you? Pick three things that represent you and explain why.

3. Write a list of 100 reasons why you are magnificent just the way you are.

4. What are characteristics that you admire in others? Why do you admire them? Where in your life have you exhibited the same characteristic? For example, you may look at someone who is very generous that gave away a lot of money. You may not have lots of money to give away, but you may have been very generous with your time.

   Keep doing this until you recognize that you have ownership of every characteristic that you admire in others within you.

5. Do you have integrity? To me, integrity is when your reputation and who you truly are, are one and the same. If not, what can you do to bring those two identities closer together?

6. What seeds are you planting in the garden of your mind? For the next day, keep a pen and paper with you at all times. Every time you notice your mind wander, make a note of what you were thinking about. Is your self-talk generally positive and hopeful, or negative and full of concern? If you find

that your self-talk is very negative, then repeat your daily mantra every time you realize you are thinking a negative thought.

7. Write down five ways that you can celebrate your crazy, unique magnificence.

FiNAL THOUGHTS

We've explored the ABCs of leadership:

- **Attitude** – Leadership has much more to do with Attitude than skill.
- **Action** – Knowledge without Action is useless, start implementing that which you already know to move toward your purpose.
- **Alliance** – Surround yourself with people who you want to learn from, those who will support you and challenge you to grow and fulfill your potential.
- **Balance** – Life is multi-dimensional, and you need many dimensions to build a solid foundation. Learn to create a healthy mix of the important areas of your life.
- **Belief** – You need to have the self-confidence to know that you can execute all the actions to make your dreams reality.
- **Behavior** – Small changes over a longer period of time can move you to any purpose.
- **Commitment** – When you truly commit to something, you find ways to overcome any obstacles that may sidetrack you.
- **Change** – Change is inevitable, but you get to choose whether you perceive it to be a positive or negative thing. Choose wisely.
- **Character** – Know who you are, celebrate who you are, and celebrate that into greatness.

Understand that this is just the tip of the iceberg when it comes to discovering what leadership is about. As I was coming up with these particular nine characteristics, it was hard for me to exclude other ABC concepts like: Animation, Building, Betterment, Choice, Challenge –

115

just to name a few. Not to mention the rest of the alphabet, there are many important concepts for strong leadership.

Leadership is different for each individual and each situation. These nine concepts should serve as a foundation for you to add other leadership characteristics that resonate with you.

You will find a theme in all of these characteristics. They are all internal. None of these elements are bought or faked. They all start from within you and are then brought to the outside world through action. You may not  have control over every set of circumstances you find yourself in, but you are in complete control of your life.

You are not a victim. You are in complete control of your response.

If you find yourself in an unfavorable situation, get out, change your perception or learn to see a benefit in that situation. Powerful leaders have no failures, just experiences that may not have been their initial outcome. As you go through the ranks of leadership, try new things. Take smart risks.

Things may not always go according to plan, but you can rest assured that if you practice the above ABCs of Leadership, you will grow stronger as a leader with each new experience you have.

Go and lead the way.

LEADERSHIP JOURNAL AND EXERCISES

1. If you have not completed your Leadership Journal and Exercises from the previous chapter, please do that first.

2. Go and repeat each exercise that you found particularly helpful.

3. Use what you have learned in this book to lead yourself to living your dreams.

ABOUT THE AUTHOR

Sunjay Nath (MBA, BScE, CSP)
www.sunjayspeaks.com

 Sunjay believes that we are all a great many things, leaders included! As a professional speaker, he travels North America sharing his insights and stories, helping students motivate themselves to achieve their goals and to get involved both in and outside of classes. He wants to spread the word that the largest hurdles that we need to overcome to achieve our goals are perhaps not where we'd expect them to be: they're often in our own minds and ingrained in our own perception of the world!

As a speaker, Sunjay has traveled extensively and addressed hundreds of thousands of people about leadership throughout North America since 1995.

Starting an international speaking business at the age of 19 was no easy task for Sunjay, especially because he wasn't even old enough to rent a car! This was particularly problematic when he would travel.

Nonetheless, years later in 2005, Sunjay became the third youngest person in the world to earn his Certified Speaking professional designation, which is the highest internationally recognized designation a speaker can achieve. He has also served as President of the Canadian Association of Professional Speakers Toronto Chapter.

Whereas speaking has been a part of his life for a great many years, Sunjay has also explored a variety of other paths along the way. He was a founding Vice President of an e-learning company based in Toronto that has gone on to become a multimillion-dollar company.

Prior to that position, he worked as an engineer for a distribution company in New York, and served as a camp director for several years at a camp that focuses on developing leadership skills in students. He has held positions with H&R Block and Bank of Montreal. In addition, Sunjay holds an undergraduate degree in Mathematical Engineering and a Masters in Business Administration. While at school, he acted as President of his Engineering Discipline.

Sunjay loves playing Ultimate Frisbee, will do anything for an afternoon nap, considers Legoland the 8th wonder of the world, and is beginning to notice that sometimes, the best ideas are found in the most unlikely of places! He has earned a Black Belt in Tae Kwon Do, has run a full 26 mile marathon and has even jumped out of a perfectly good plane (some call it skydiving).

He is a magician, a comedian, a professional actor; he can juggle and he was rated as one of the country's top debaters. With his background, Sunjay offers a rare combination of both left and right brain activities that will keep all audience members captivated and laughing.

If you have questions, comments or are interested in booking Sunjay for a speaking event you can contact him at sunjay@sunjaynath.com.

NOTES

NOTES

NOTES

NOTES